D0123610

Checkered Mates

Checkered Mates

Poems by

Tricia Knoll

Thank you for
your ongoing
encouragement,
mate

Tricia

© 2021 Tricia Knoll. All rights reserved.
This material may not be reproduced in any form, published,
reprinted, recorded, performed, broadcast,
rewritten or redistributed without
the explicit permission of Tricia Knoll.
All such actions are strictly prohibited by law.

Cover design by Shay Culligan

ISBN: 978-1-954353-13-8

Kelsay Books
502 South 1040 East, A-119
American Fork, Utah, 84003

To those to whom I've been a queen.
To those to whom I've seemed a pawn.
To the few who know me as a knight.

Contents

Defining Checkered Mates—Multiple-Choice

A. Australian mates range from an impoverished widower from the same side of your freeway who paints houses gray to the girl with salmon-pink socks from your third-year French class. A mate is not necessarily the person with whom you bed down.

B. Imagine a frayed red-and-white tablecloth. Sunburned hands sop up pinot noir on an August picnic table. You are sitting in unspoken sympathy with a friend's story of how she was raped. You also think of the black teenager whom police shot last night.

C. Visualize a jump from a red to a black square. You're chasing kings, risking loss of pawn-power. The doorbell rings, your spaniel knocks over an aspidistra, smashing a green Shawnee pot.

D. Those crosshatched cracks in the concrete commons that will break your mother's back—if you step on moss, do you believe you hurt her?

E. Hugging a former husband in front of neighbors known for gossip.

F. The bullied teenager you admire who hangs himself two weeks after graduation.

G. The retired banker who leaves out one-eighth of a cup of antifreeze for his neighbor's barking beagle.

H. Moving toward candlelit lovemaking on a stormy January night. The power company hotline insists lights may come on any minute. A squirrel fried in the rigging. Neither lover remembers which switches are flipped on, which off.

I. A brain hiccough bigger than when one spouse spells checkered, the other chequered. More like when well-worn, stable plaids of relationship go zigzag, one squabble off-kiltering another.

J. Do you seek the robot petting zoo to keep your loneliness a secret?

All of the above?

None?

The Barista's View of Winter through
Condensation on the Coffee House Window

Those two come in separately once a week, mid-afternoon
on Thursdays when the weather is unpleasant.
I know his order—a caramel macchiato in an it's-too-hot
sleeve, no whipped cream. She wants decaf lattes.
I know their first names which is more
than they know of each other. They call me Sue.

Today he wears a Red Sox cap and stares
at the blackboard. He never orders a panini
or curried tofu salad. I start the spitting espresso
to create his perfect palm leaf of foam.

She sets up her guitar next to the steamed window
that blurs the piles of black slush the plow left.
She moves her scarred stool, preparing for more gospel
trains, cats in the cradle and the silver spoon.
I give her a non-fat heart.

While she fiddles the dial on her amp, he opens
a Sudoku paperback. She bows her head, tunes.
Her ashy hair tumbles. Her knee jigs an old denim skirt

she probably wore as a hippy. Minor chords lift
up what's left of her repertoire,
folk tunes of red poppies, fleeing unicorns,
double-edged swords and sleeping rough
in the devil's bed.

He puts a buck in her bowl, nods at me.
He stage whispers he's sick of sad songs. At least,
he mutters, she who sleeps in the devil's bed
does not sleep alone.

Amen, I say.
I have devils of my own.

Solace

Jerry saw the silhouette of his father's face
in the naked branches of the oak.
That was how he knew his father
would be at hand through winter.
The father who took him to the park
to see dragons and tractors in storm clouds.

His brother brought pepperoni pizza,
not enough for the retired teachers
who showed up with deviled eggs
or the aging men with motorcycles drinking
beer by the curb. His neighbor Lou
was kind enough to say he saw the face
even though he insisted those arriving
should park their cars inside the lines
while they unbuckled children and hugged
as if they hadn't seen their cousins
three weeks ago at the ninetieth
birthday party where the now dead
patriarch had praised the frosted green cake
for his Irish wife he said he planned
to see again soon. That night he blew
out nine wavering candles with such vigor
that Jerry thought he might live
forever or at least to ninety-one.

Now that face in limbs. Jerry stands
on the curb, looks west where sunset
backlights the oak. The laughing lip is right,
the add-on tuft of scraggle beard. By midnight
Jerry decides to remain silent about the likeness

hovering in that tornado-twisted oak.
No one expects Jerry to nurture the family
as his father did with stories mixing truth
and hyperbole, humor and righteousness.
It was enough to not be left alone.

Dali's Clock

Maria rolls time like a roulette wheel.
How many days has she celebrated Christmas?
She claims one hundred. I know it's less.
She uncovers gin in a hiding hole
and it's cocktail hour.

Why wait to thank God on Friday?
Flickering candles for her dead son
or the overlap when a cabbie drives
her to the grand casino for slots?
Time sneaks about in dotted lines
like ants on her kitchen counter.

I bought an enormous clock—
large letters with the day, date, year and time,
and picked off gummy Alzheimer
labels. Cling, I hoped, to this anchor
one day at a time even as directions

drift. South, an abstraction
of bougainvillea, Fidel Castro,
old Havana, the Prado.
Tumbling on Tenth Street,
(she calls it First), swollen fingers
strangle her walker.

If she falls again, wading in a muddy river
of has-had secrets, if she trips on cobbles
she suspects we set, if she falls,
she knows she must move.

The landlord leaves her toilet paper in the hall.
She hesitates to open the door. New people
every month, while the hall smells of old people.
And the clock, the damn clock, she yells,
keeps sliding off her wall.

Yes, I'm Cissy Bales

Yes, I locked up Guilt in the north barn stall.
Yes, I nailed a 2×4 across the latch
and tacked up rusty barbed wire.
Understand. She arrived scratched
and naked, says she'd been raped,
her money gone on drugs. She claims
she has no one but me.

I can't stand her filthy hands, stringy hair.
I gave her socks, jeans, stout boots, a cape,
a brush—she says no one has ever been so good.

She sat at my kitchen window watching
the level of my gin bottle—looking
for bad guys out to get even.
She weighs my trash and hisses
at my cat. Her you're-screwing-up mantra
points blame eight times. She hums like a cello
that bites and gripes in my bad ear at night.
She curdles my dreams. When I try to move her,
she vanishes—from that small stall.
Where to? Under the saddle blankets,
into the hay. Out of the way. I don't know!

She needs little, impossibly little.
Yes, she nibbles fallen oats
like a rat at chicken scratch.
She licks drips from the eaves
and bathes in the goat trough.

I don't know where Guilt is now,
how you heard she's here,
or when she's coming back.

This is not elder abuse. I'm doing
what any normal person would do.

Un-Mooning the Moon

The moon's scoured silver slides over our bedroom's Persian rug.
The gray cat streaks out an open screen door to the June woods.

We, the longing lovers, wrapped in sheets of disbelief,
uncertain, pay no attention to silent cat scurry
or rustlings in blue violets. We have truths
to attend to. Or I do.

This light shines false. That moon no more cradles us
than it comforts soldiers in sour trenches, covers the stench
of gangrenous flesh with jasmine or protects hollow
helmets in shadows cast from brittle leafless trees.

Now you snore. I embrace bare facts.
Low-slung, the lunar face is acned styrofoam.
A dead man glares at us with cratered eyes. The moon rabbit
in a basalt robe dances between blasted sockets.
Diana's hunt over this woods ends with archer arms
crashing on the brindled floor.
Kwan Yin's crescent fails to hold rising tides
at bay. Such warm seas rise and storms surge.

My cat screams.

Out the open door,
I call for her under this vagrant moon
—my flashlight finds the cat's head
where the coyote chucked it.

Moon mist rises
                    and falls
cursed spite
                    on human sight

this dim lamp light   even for cat eyes.

Harvest at Ghost Ranch, Abiquiu, New Mexico

The farmhand cranks up his baler. The rake lifts
drying grass, scraped from silver dust.
He drags rows, makes rectangles
smaller and smaller inside themselves.

You and I smell gray-green.
Fall's clumping, a distraction
of gold and cider, last berries and spiders,
the death of dahlias, the dog's shed of summer.
The baler extrudes perfect block bales.

On wood chairs below gold cottonwoods we share
strategies for the dialogue poem you wrote
to the woman who deserted you, kidnapped your dog
and stole what you believe was your last chance

at love. I note ambiguities of blame
you assign to mothers, yours who named
you for a nun and said nuns never lied,
hers who was careless with knives

and believed all her daughter's lies.
I suggest stanza breaks for each speaker.
Two men with a green truck stack bales
like books on a cart. You remove your glasses,

wipe them. In this dust of honest harvest,
you weep. The truck sways under its load.
I know where it goes. To barns sheltering
winter's steam-breathers, hope curling

from the nostrils of impatient horses,
and the tackling antics of restless goats
for a place at the manger. I've seen it delivered.

Detailing

I'd detail you if I knew how.
Your shine needs a buff
and if you welcome it, rubbing.

Which, of course, you wouldn't
want a dangling pine-tree deodorizer,
a gleaming bumper,

or a rear-view mirror
aimed to see me
as I think I am.

Lament of the Heirloom Red Deer Tongue Lettuce

You never understood
  what I need to grow.

A fine bed, enriched
  with patience.

Wait for a warm moment,
  do not rush rosettes.

Push seed in the depth of an eyelash,
    restraint.

Leaven with earthiness,
  long-time compost.

Water with an even hand
  my red-tipped tongue.

Brush dust from my ruffles.
  Wait again. Wait.

Thin with delicacy, make room
  for midribs, my round tips.

Take me in my time
    field-ripe, full laced.

Had this been your way with me,
    I would not have bolted.

For Buzz

Your woman carves cedar masks
and walks her dogs with loose leashes.
You wished she cooked the goose
or duck you shot *a la chinoise.*
She didn't make you a mask
until she formed your death mask,
her special request to the coroner
who wanted to see some paperwork
to permit plaster and scraps to embrace
your lips. Documentation that your brother
wouldn't mind, your father gone.
She was the best friend you had.
Maybe you wouldn't have hung yourself
in the attic if you could have realized
how much she loved you, duck or no duck.

Heartbreak

A friend called it the foundering of a mighty white-winged horse,
limping through mossy damp. Wounded. Untamable.

He was wrong. There is no such thing as heartbreak.
The heart curdles, congeals, skedaddles in bad beats.

If it broke, we would die—
heartbreak is not so kind.

It gallops a deafening drum song
or taps at windows with bony fingers,

but never, ever does it break open
the way love does.

Two Poets in the Weight Room

Verlena carries a black cane. I have lumpy veins.
Our ages add up to nearly a gross of years
in this hotbed of stair steps, elliptical and
rowing machines, barbells, mirrors, and sweat.

Neither of us has stomach
for the maiming news on silenced TVs
or a captioned chef stuffing wieners
with cheddar cheese. I flaunt red
nails on heart-monitoring handlebars.
She wears a red sweatshirt. We show up.

I suggest we hang out for the firefighters'
free gym access at eleven. They are cuter
than the upper-chest guy pumping up
to dazzle skinny boy learning squats.
Verlena lays down her cane, leans
on the upper-back torture rack.
She laments that no one guesses
she eyes groins and puffed-out pecs.

Doing lat pulls, I huff out how much I admire
tight-spanked butts when stuck in traffic, those men
in two-tone bike shorts zipping up the right lane,
the swervy audacity of steel-strung calves
on sculpted seats.

The firefighters never come. Something burns.
The two lifters trade hints on mixing slow counts
with heavy reps.

We flesh out odes. They count haiku.

Moving the Queen

All she wanted when she fled up
north was to keep her child and man—
she hummed her starlight song all along.

All she wanted from Mother's Day
was for her son and another
mother's boy to let each other live.

All she wanted from her locked chain
on the White House fence was to vote
in an election for President.

All she wanted from a wheelchair
rolling her body to the voter's booth
was a death with dignity.

All she wants running for office
is to oust the jerks that tell her
to do more with less and love it.

All she wants from her website
is for Muslim and Jewish women
to read each other's poetry.

All she wants from a pink t-shirt
is to walk with womenfolk
who celebrate survival.

All she wants from bumper stickers
is for neighbors to know
she will marry Isabelle.

All she wants to find online
is work that lets her feed her twins
more than macaroni and cheese.

All I want holding the queen
is to slide her fleet-foot fury
to checkmate the cross-head king.

Uniformed Man on the Dike in New Orleans

To get where we were, stuck in the Ninth Ward
on top of the new rock levee required
a plastic ID for National Guard checkpoints.
He had one; I had one, responders
on an October day on a New Orleans dike.
Red plastic roses sagged on a porch
that had no house.
We couldn't be strangers,
there was too little else of living.

My agency was helping restore
drinking water to New Orleans,
righting toppled hydrants,
reconnecting shattered mains.
His eyes cast about like cats
after a storm, blue like this beat-down sky
in high humidity. He wore a hot black shirt
and carried bottled water.

He spoke of his bagging company,
contractors who come after dogs
sniff out remains in rubble
and someone spray paints the doors
orange. D-Mort people who extract wholes
or pieces, bag them, and carry
them to freezer cars.

He had worked 9-11, the plains in Pennsylvania,
the Oklahoma bombing, Hurricane Andrew, now Katrina.
He looked at his hands, at the scummy water
below the dike, and at me. If he found me somewhere,
I'd be happy to have his hands handle me.

This kind of kind man when he retires
does not tell stories
                    of the good old days.

Ode to the Postcard

Little card, I know you don't want to hear about it,
that fleeting word—e-mail. You who knows
that every story has two sides,
even *wish you were here, I miss you,*
and *thank you for your kindness over tea.*
You bear extra-special images of antique
roses, Wyoming's wonky jackalope,
Inuit line art of the whale, or the photos
of motorized skates and Escher's waterfall
from the Museum of Impractical Devices.
Oh, I love your flimsiness that invites
my right hand to scrawl with no fear
of the fingerprint of delete.
Go ahead—invite the postal person
in the small white truck to flip you
over as if you are a pancake
destined for a drool of maple syrup.
You carry codes between lovers,
like my oblique phrase about dachshunds.
I scribble to intrigue the letter carrier
who usually approaches hard-knock mail slots
and arched sheet-metal boxes, wary
of the mad dog, to sling ads
for grocer's sales or water bills.
When all is said and you drop
through the slot to the vestibule floor,
go ahead—reinvent yourself
as a bookmark in the bodice-ripper
parked beside the unmade bed.

Late Afternoon Fall Tea with My Daughter

I can't decide whether to mention
what is stuck in my head, glued in yesterday—
this is my last fall. A premonition
because leaves jump ship? A worry
not about knee scabs, but death?

I silence fortunetelling, treating this
moment like the very best it is,
two of us warm in sun through the window.

Her hands punctuate stories of two cousins visiting
New York, summer's jostled hovercraft ride
on the Snake, my grandmother's jade ring lost
in community garden compost. She folds one leaf
from my maple to the size of a dime.

I cannot read her palm lines even if I knew how,
so much gesture in her telling.

The kettle works to bring up a boil.
I choose a rose verbena mix, pour
and fill my mother's green teapot.

Mine is the blue-and-white willow cup;
she takes my water utility mug.
Outside, more redbud heart-leaves
hesitate, flicker, wait to jump.

She shifts the storyline to a casual date
with a man much her senior, a colleague
but not close enough to cause problems.

After the tea steeps, I don't let flakes
float free to rain in cups. I strain them.
I cannot pretend to read leaves
and neither can she.

Simple Signs & Messages

What does not kill us makes us stronger.
—*Friedrich Nietzsche*

That graffiti spray-painted on plywood after Katrina—
a busty woman in a blue dress points to a future
of muddy plywood and twisted jeans sodden in oily water.
Some artist believed Nietzsche

like I believe in postcards, hundreds I've sent,
bought at our thrift store—cast-off postcards.
Eighteen cents each. Florida flamingos,
Outer Banks beaches, a bald eagle, the Museum
of African American History & Culture, a humpback
breaching in the Tongass, moon over Hokkaido
—and so many others

for legislators.
Shine light on healthcare. (Presque Isle Light.)
Keep public lands forested. (Mt. Hood from Lolo Pass.)
Support diversity and refugees. (Amish buggy at sunset.)
Protect veterans. (Tennessee State Veteran Home.)
Make us stronger in love. (Fanny Brawne's house in Hampstead.)

Make us stronger in love.

Wooing the Dog

You think I love you because of how you are with my dog.
You let her lick your lips.
You think putting gefilte fish on her kibble
   earns you a place in paradise.

When both of you are naked bathing
with a squeaky rubber ducky,
you're sure a dog-loving woman will follow
into hot water. Still you fill the water bowl.

Because my dog heels with a nose at your knee,
you believe we are hooked up.
You laugh at the rotten-fur golf club cover
   the mutt drags from the mud puddle
   to shake and strangle with the fury of the furred.
You save a last bite of everything for her,
   from sirloin to mango curry.
I take any last bite I want.

It's easy for you to slip her out of her blue collar.
How readily I shed my clothes for you.
You whistle. I come, running.
You wait for my tail to wag.
Brown eyes beg. Stroke me.
Fondle my deep ears.
Take a bite of my milk bone.
You who woo the dog woo me.

Label Warnings I Didn't Read

I shrunk a green cotton dress
before I got too fat to wear it.

Despite a diagram for how the ink fits
in the printer, I press forward with intuition.

When the amber check-engine light comes on,
I wait too long to drive to the mechanic's shop.

I forgot to beat the egg whites
for Belgian waffles. Twice.

Today I planted the new Go-To-Gold
rose beside last year's prize-winning pink.

Then I read the tag, *this rose
is not comfortable with pastels.*

You said you didn't think I could change you.
I didn't know you came with a tag

that said *I cannot be any other way,*
attached with a wire on your root stock,

wary of pastels.

The Usefulness of an Umbrella

Few care about this ordinariness
that spends summer days in the back of closets
until a chiller wind whips in squalls and out of nowhere
you are on a city street with the only person you can imagine
sharing with, an uneven compromise of broad shoulders
and slim expectations or steps bumbled in fear of falling
and his hand is so much bigger than yours. If
this were a seesaw, you'd wonder if it is play,
a tug and release, let me take care of you instead
of taking care of myself so wholeheartedly that I let go
or diminish myself so our ceiling is higher and broader
and perhaps darker under the onslaught of showers.

What you know is that umbrellas are precarious:
they turn inside out and ribs poke through vulnerable
spaces. Sharp. A latch breaks and the expected upside
falls down like a veil and you no longer see everything
as you should, muddled in furled drapery. The friend
goes another way, steps into the Uber going uptown
and you are certainly downtown. Too much rain
is falling to leave semi-useful behind and yet you do,
declaring the broken as discard, seeking
the trash can that swallows the thing whole
until you can find the shop that sells another one—
perhaps purple with bright gold stars.

Letter to My First Husband Written during Surgery in Which He Was Transformed into a Woman

An old man in a Grace Paley story advises that to age well, take your heart in both hands every morning when you wake up. Talk to it. Supply words to further the work it needs to do.

Your surgeon makes intricate folds and tucks, the rightness you seek. May he have the skill of your mother, the seamstress. When finished, take your heart into both hands. And your breasts. Talk to them. Touch your new vagina. Whisper healing.

You have always been smart. When your eyes focused on a distance, I knew you were off being smart somewhere. Sometimes you would share, but mostly you didn't. How could you explain what it's like to stare at a nameless star?

It stands to reason that you would jump to the best. To join the demographic that lives the longest … old ladies. A by-right-of-long-lasting, the lonely majority who accepts invisibility. Invisible to the men who smell of cigarette smoke and sell chocolate bars in gas stations or the university students who break the ice shells on frozen puddles with their heavy-heeled boots. They don't know what wild once beat in our hearts.

You are wise to join us. We need all the smart ones we can assemble. I didn't realize that the young protesters in Hong Kong carried umbrellas to avoid being identified in security cameras. I thought monsoon season had hit Hong Kong big time.

Every person lugs an identity umbrella. You've put an ill-equipped one aside. (Mine matches the onesie that our grandson wears.) Choose a new fabric. Swirl in rainbow choices. We may not need umbrellas this minute, but they come in handy in the face of deluges and idiots.

Waiting these dark hours for news of your surgery's progress feels like standing by for a baby to be born. Bless the newborn grandmother.

Waiting for My First Husband to Get Off the Plane

In the airport lounge I was too tired to consider
expectation. Planes from the west arrive past dinner
on the east coast—I anticipated your hunger.
Going cross-country requires more
than potato chips, grapes and cheese wedges.
I was conjuring jet lag, the squeeze
of airplane seats, bad air, a crying kid,
the passenger in the next seat who sneezes.
That's what I was imagining, not
this new you, you arriving
in a blue dress with white flowers
that made sense on you.
Now I worry about your bare legs
in the chill of this on-its-way winter.

Relativity of Loss

Although not one of my men would accuse me of carelessness,
I have lost much of what each gave me. I long for the photo
of my father's German Shepherd whose front paws hung
from the crotch of an oak. In a black-frame.

Or on the hill outside your mother's house,
you say you asked, "Will you marry me?" How can I have lost
all recollection, all sense of that, knowing what your Jewish Afro
looked like, what your stiff beard felt like against my chin.
I suspected that marriage would not have worked, but to have been
young and pretty—and forget my first marriage proposal?

I can't guess where the ring is from my first marriage. His Aries
symbol, my Scorpio, etched in solid 14K gold, simple hippy rings
we each wore for twenty years. Maybe melted
into dangles or a rabbit-shaped pin.

That tiniest of Nootka baskets, the one the old woman wove
of sweet grass from the west beach of Vancouver Island.
I gave it to my next lover, and he lost it,
that smell of fresh I thought would last forever.
Perhaps it's in a trunk with his other untouchables—
his brother's journal, the painting of his mother.

I made the decision to lose my uterus, the sense of which
these men conceived, shook into splendor, or enriched
to birth a baby. I made the decision to hysterectomy.
That's how it's different.

One at a Time

The teenage girl told male voices in sing-songy rhyme
to leave by her window, pronto, one at a time.

Her mother, thinking her both schitzy and ditzy,
advised loving a man, assumed one at a time.

The girl drank wine and beer, moved up to gin,
learned to make gold margaritas one lime at a time.

She learned to love men, five or six in total,
depending if you count only one at a time.

She had three husbands, from most perspectives
it worked out sequentially one at a time.

Not as easy to get pregnant as her mother had said,
she worked with her doctor, asked for one at a time.

At thirty she heard voices of babies she lost,
hope-blood of miscarriages, sad ones each time.

Now raspy old voices stand in line as she grays,
their advice insists this be her very last time

to paint retablos of friends, moments
of moony remembrance she mourns one at a time.

She walks in red dust to her end of days.
This crone begs muse-winds, *speak one at a time.*

Basketry

As though regret
was not a waste
but a basket
loosely woven
passed from pew
to pew for fingers
to drop in bits
to support
a greater good.

As though regret
was a sieve
for catching pith
and pulp of oranges
to let juice
rain through.

As wine settles,
aged in oak
becomes
the fitter drink.

Walking Matrimonial Trail in New Mexico Alone

A man from town promised that I could not get lost
taking this trail from one side of the ranch to the other.
He advised that you meet me at the other end.
Start north of the cattle guard. Slog up
a double-rutted wagon trail, a gutter-wash
to flash-flood rains. Two could ascend
as equals, side by side, skirt deep red dust
the horses churned. Some blue boulders.
Two grandiose anthills. Dry chemisa bloom.
A view unfolds back to the reservoir, the plateau,
that hill of flint—Cerro Pedernal.

A mile on, the trail swells. A circle site
for attendants, where a ministrant
might drone reassuring vows.
A soft wind dries the sweat of climb.
A smell of commitment, blue asters.
sage and nodding grasses. I stop,
given over. Reminisce where love brought me—
switchbacks to a vista of rock striped
white, blue, adobe red, and light-gold sandstone.

Hold still long enough for a ceremony.
Then move on. The trail thins to a tightrope,
slopes, slants to a long, long way down.

I brace against where fear of drop-offs
battles twins of will and curiosity.
Fright wins. I turn. Begin to retrace the hot hike
back to the faded wood sign at the road. Each step
stirs a memory of wedded failure—his sore eye,
large hands that pound piano keys, a green pick-up truck,
and canned spaghetti mixed with scrambled eggs.

I have done this all my life.
Backtracked matrimonial trails.
Reversed when going gets tough.
My cell phone catches a tower.
I tell you. My fear. I cannot meet you
on the other side.
As some third marriages work,
you get it.

Timing

A twist of sunlight insists I go back to when it began,
to that orange you tossed through an open window
onto my desk littered with writing that wanted to be
important but was as flimsy as night air, as thin

as our first kiss outside a door in a cooling-off fall,
or your whistle below a metal window, a memory
stunning in the way of the cardinal's happiness
this June morning.

May blessings be in what's remembered from best,
from simple times your bike followed mine
as we weaved among the eucalyptus with our books
flopping in canvas bags to long embraces in airports.

My dogs rest in the grass, one in shade, one in sun
until the sunny one flips onto her back and rolls on
her aching spine, just enough to rejoice—like the day
she chased a cranky rooster and shut him up.

That kindness of getting old. If you have enough
days, you can choose to remember when good
outweighed sad. The orange so ripe my fingers dripped
sweet and that dog's pride in tearing apart the bird.

Frigatebird

Awake with half my brain
to your sadness, woe
a sea you cannot cross,
cannot rest in for fear
of letting the mirror
of heavy water
pull you under.
Wings that will not
land. Not this day.

Awake I carry you
with half my brain,
part of the sun
of mid-day;

the other wonders
exactly where you fly,
what thermal lifts you,
waking or dreaming.

The bird that mates
for life.

How to Bless

In Old English etymology, the word blessing began with sprinkling blood on a pagan altar—a hint of messy demands. The heart requires lessons to learn the way of it. Quiet thankfulness floats by faster than a cloud of malaise. Ecstasy is not a call to action. Blessing is an act of volition.

Reliability and consistency are clues to when to invoke blessing. A second-hand station wagon with a dented door that drives fine. The seatbelts work. The sonnet that holds up to five readings. Friends who show up. Trustworthy mates.

Watch for disguised blessings. A robust woman with a veil over scars. The lemon smell of the gold rose. An extended wait for the diagnosis that nothing is wrong. Death offering escape.

Yesterday, browned-out moss on the labyrinth path greened up after a shower—not a rain that ended drought—only drizzle that changed the color of things. A soft sound. That blood on the pagan altar.

How a Woman Kisses a Ghost She Knows

I approach this as any woman might, a bit virginal.
Palm to palm, a forehead nod as if Buddha waits.

Expect no cheek offered. Go lipstick-less.
Print no more red marks on the dead.

Do not force another mitzvah of washing,
even one you are willing to perform.

If you have not forgiven, offer an index finger first,
point toward a ceiling of uncertain outcome.

If you have forgiven, walk as if your toes tingle
and your knees know their backsides.

Swirl your hands like waltzing, as if you mean
to sculpt voluptuousness. Keep gloves out of sight.

Lick your lips. Be shy. Words may not be necessary
or accurate.

Acknowledgments

Thank you to these journals and anthologies that initially published versions of the following pieces:

Calyx: "Dali's Clock"

Columbia Journal Online: "The Barista's View of Winter through Condensation on the Coffee House Window," "Yes, I'm Cissy Bales"

Courtship of Wind: "Basketry"

Halfway Down the Stairs: "Lament of Heirloom Red Deer Tongue Lettuce"

Is the Moon a World? (Osedax & Scrimschander Press Anthology): "Un-Mooning the Moon"

Montana Mouthful: "Walking Matrimonial Trail in New Mexico Alone"

Peacock Journal: "Warnings on the Label I Did Not Read," "Simple Signs & Messages"

Rivet: "How a Woman Kisses a Ghost She Knows"

San Diego Poetry Annual 2014–2015: "The Relativity of Loss"

Verse Virtual: "Solace," "The Usefulness of an Umbrella"

Visitant: "How to Bless"

VoiceCatcher: "Two Poets in the Weight Room"

Willawaw Journal: "Frigatebird"

About the Author

Tricia Knoll is a Vermont poet who sometimes feels she has learned most of what she knows the hard way. She is deeply grateful for family, poet friends, and mentors who contributed to her learning. And the two dogs of the pandemic. Mates in the deep sense.

Her work appears widely in journals and anthologies and has received nine Pushcart nominations and one Best of Net. Her chapbook *Urban Wild* (Finishing Line Press) focuses on interactions between wildlife and humans in urban habitat. *Ocean's Laughter* (Aldrich Press) details change over time, both personal and environmental, in the small coastal town of Manzanita, Oregon. *Broadfork Farm* (The Poetry Box) highlights the creatures and people of a small organic farm in Trout Lake, Washington where Knoll was a regular farmsitter. How *I Learned To Be White* (Antrim House) details Knoll's exploration of the impact of white privilege in her family background, education, and growing awareness of racial inequality. *How I Learned To Be White* received the 2018 Indie Book Award for Motivational Poetry.

Before coming out as a poet (printing a business card), Knoll studied literature at Stanford University (BA) and Yale University (MAT). She taught high school English for ten years, killing Julius Caesar in a classroom some twenty-two times. From there she went on to Public Relations for Portland, Oregon's Children Museum; and served as the Public Information Officer for the Portland Water Bureau—writing the staples of a water utility and wishing they were poetry. She was a FEMA-trained emergency responder to Hurricane Katrina.

She has spasmodic dysphonia, a neurological speech glitch, that gives her a healthy respect for silence and dogs who understand her every word.

Made in the USA
Monee, IL
28 March 2021

63118549R00031